THE INGENIOUS RAMBLINGS
OF A
MADMAN

BY
MIRAKULUZ

This is a work of fiction. Names, characters, places, and incidents are either the product of the author's imagination or are used fictitiously. However, this was written to hit home with a lot of people, so if there happens to be a scenario you can relate to, don't get mad. Be happy someone understands.

An UnLabeled Entertainment Release

Copyright 2007 Johnny Conley

Written by Johnny "Mirakuluz" Conley

Any reproduction or duplication of this book is strictly prohibited without the expressed written consent of UnLabeled Entertainment.

ISBN 978-0-6151-8071-7

DEDICATED TO MY SON

JAVION DINARD CONLEY

AND TO EVERYONE THAT WANTS TO CHANGE THE WORLD

TABLE OF CONTENTS

PRELUDE

FUNNY SIDE

WHEN I WOKE UP THIS MORNING

YESTERDAY

NERVES

SHOOKUP

YESTERDAY: CONTINUED (THE EXAMPLE)

PISSED OFF

RETIRED NIGGER

GOTTA GO

TRAVELIN'

BRAINSTORM

NO WAY HOME

GETTING GONE

VACANCY (BASS HEAD)

DREAMS (IN TECHNICOLOR)

NO CONTINENTAL BREAKFAST

COLD COFFEE

ANOTHER BRAINSTORM

MR. G-MAN

HUSTLING

HUSTLING: PART 2

SUNSHINE

YOU'RE BEAUTIFUL

THE ISLE OF A THOUSAND SMILES

SUCTION

RAMBLIN' WITH AN OLD SOUL
A NATURAL REMEDY
LISTEN: BE YOU!
LOOK AT HIM (GOD)
OUTCASTIN'
EBONY TREES
INFINITE LIMITLESS
THE INGENIOUS RAMBLINGS
RAMBLE ON, YOUNG MAN

PRELUDE

So, I see that you've stumbled upon my Journal of Rambled Thoughts. Oh no, don't put them down. I don't mind sharing them. In fact, I was thinking about sharing some of my ramblings with people anyway. Whether amused or intrigued, people always seemed interested in my writings. The only difference is, now I'm not afraid to share them because of fear of what others may say or think. Every thought has a purpose, and every word has a reason. It's just up to you to discover its meaning.

Who am I? Oh, I apologize. Let me introduce myself. I'm Jay. And the papers you hold in your hand come from my journal. Sometimes, I write down events that happen throughout my day, and other times I just write random thoughts that pop into my mind. But, at the end of the day, they all seem to mesh in one ingenious way.

So go ahead, read those. In fact, you can keep them. They may entail a message or thought that can not only help you today, but help you in your future. Please enjoy my ramblings, as some will take them as fallacies, but sooner or later, they will be received as reality.

THE FUNNY SIDE OF LIFE

Whoever wakes up from a dream and can't seem to tell the difference between the dream and the reality had seen the funny side of life. When you can no longer dine off of information from the ones around you because they're still eating leftovers and you're ready for a new entrée has seen the funny side of life. When you open your mouth and speak a truth that suddenly boiled up inside of you, yet no one around you can decipher its message, you have seen the funny side of life. I, too, have seen this side of life before. In fact, I see it now. I live in it.

Ever since I found the key to that side of the brain people are scared to unlock, I've been there. Ever since I walked downtown and saw dozens and dozens of entertainers, yet the only stars I saw were in the sky, I've been there. Ever since someone told me about the latest escapades of the newest young actor or actress and I replied, "So?" I have been there. An outcast, some say I am. So it may seem to you as well, but really I'm not. I just changed my address from the common life of the monogamous mind to the funny side of life, where thoughts are seen in 3-D on HDTV, and words are as thick and as filling as homemade steak and potatoes. Where you are whoever you say you are, and no one can copy or clone you. No one can judge you because your way of thinking isn't on their tiny mental atlas. Where your dreams are as real as the nose on your face, and the only thing that is impossible is failure. Where everyone speaks in spoken word, they let out their emotions in songs, and they all write their signatures in graffiti. I welcome you to the funny side of life.

WHEN I WOKE UP THIS MORNING

When I woke up this morning, the sun rays slowly opened my eyes. I thought to myself, "Thank God, I'm still alive". I buried my face in the pillow, but I couldn't find that spot of comfort anymore. I looked over at the clock; it read 9:34. It was earlier than I thought, but, for the first time in a long time, I didn't toss and turn in my sleep. I guess my mind, body, and soul worked as one because the dream I had was so deep. I hadn't had a dream like this in years because it's hard to dream when you sleep with one eye open. Yet, this dream was so surreal, just the hope in it nearly made me wake up hoping. Have you ever had a dream so realistic, you woke up wondering if it really happened? The truth in it was so refreshing, when you woke up you were nearly saddened? That's exactly how it was, like that kiss from that model on your wall, or that huge bank statement, or that infamous "we need you to save the world" phone call. Let me tell you my dream.

There I stood,
Surrounded by darkness so thick,
It'll take a steak knife to cut thru it.
I couldn't see what was two inches in front of me,
I could barely even breathe,
All I could hear was moaning and wailing from every direction,
But I had no clue what was in front or in back of me.
I was so frightened that I began to sweat,
Yet it felt like blood was pouring from my pores,
And it burned like someone had poured alcohol into my sores.
I yelled for someone to help me,
But my cries seemed to fall on the ears of the deaf,
So I came to the conclusion that I would have to help myself.
I dug into my pocket
And pulled out my old pocket knife,

I opened it up, grabbed a hold of some of the darkness,
And I began to slice.
I sliced and sliced and the more I sliced the darker it seemed to get.
And the wailing and groaning got louder and louder,
And my arm felt as though it was bit,
And I felt grimy claws grab for me,
And sharp teeth pierce my skin,
But no matter what I continued to slice,
I would not give in.
And as I sliced I finally struck what seemed to be a wall,
So I climbed and climbed,
But my foot slipped and I began to fall.
I feel hard upon the ground,
And screamed because my back was sore,
But I quickly got back to my feet,
And began to climb some more.
There was darkness all around me,
And creatures clawing and gnawing at me left and right,
But I would not succumb to it,
I continued to fight.
I climbed and climbed and finally I reached the wall's peak,
But I couldn't see what was on the other side,
So, out of faith, I just leaped.
I leaped to the other side and let out a loud yell,
My body was falling like a plane out the sky
As my lungs filled with air,
I fell thru the darkness,
Not worried at all if I might crash,
I leaped out of faith and kept my faith until there was a loud
SPLASH!!!!

I had landed in water so I grabbed hold to a log that was in reach,

I pulled my head above the water to realize
I was at the beach.
How'd I get here?
A beautiful beach with clear water,
A bright blue sky and white sand on the shore,
Such a magnificent sight that I had never seen before.
There were men and women on the beach,
All of them smiling so happy and free,
And right then I had made up my mind this is were
I wanted to be.
I walked up to a sunbathing woman
And I said, "Hi. My name is Jay, and I was wondering,
Where am I?"
She said that I was in the place that I had struggled so hard to reach,
And everyone here was living in Perfect Peace.
I asked her how I could stay here forever,
I just knew it'll cost big bucks,
She said I could stay for free,
All that I had to do was
WAKE UP.

And as soon as she said that, I did. The dream was beautiful, but that's all it was: a dream. I guess it's time for me now to think on more realistic things. I know there was a message in the dream, and that's cool, but sometimes, no matter how good your intentions are, you're still played as the fool. Take yesterday for example...

YESTERDAY (THE EXAMPLE)

I went to work with the mindset that I just wasn't going to complain about my job anymore. I was going to work hard! I was going to give service with a smile, and that was that. My job had recently hired some new big wigs at the top, and they were pissing everyone off, including me. I had worked at this same meat-packing factory for nearly two years. It was the same thing every day; cut the meat, wrap it in plastic. If the meat is a little old or questionable, trim off as much of the bad as possible, and make sure the good side is facing upwards. That's it. It was simple as pie, but too simple for me. I wanted to move into sales. They made more money, and the interaction with people is something I looked forward to. After a while, you get tired of looking at the same melancholy faces and smelling meat all the time. None of the meat-cutters were happy. We all hated the new bosses, we all hated our pay, and we all hated our lives. I had to get away from that.

About a week ago, a position in sales opened up. I was excited. I just knew it was meant for me. So I applied for it with the confidence that I was going to get that job and that was going to be the answers to all my prayers. And yesterday, after a week of knowing that my days as a meat-cutter were nearly done, my thoughts became true. Just not how I thought it would happen.

After a whole day working hard, cutting meat and freestyling rhymes in my mind to myself, I was ready to go home and relax a little. As I grabbed my things and headed to the door, one of the new big wigs stopped me.

"Jay, can we have a quick word with you?" he asked. I just knew it was about the sales position.

"Alright, sure," I replied with a huge grin. We walked into the office area of the factory and into the main board room. Along the way, we passed by the empty sales desk, the same position I had applied for. I envisioned myself in a suit, sitting in the comfortable chair with one of those telephone earpieces, chopping it up with a potential customer. I just knew that job was mine. When I got to the office, he sat me down in a chair in front of a long table.

"Wait right here for one second while I go get the others." As he walked away, I knew something wasn't right. Several employees looked at me as if I was on death row or something. One of the big wigs came into the room, and stared at me. He didn't say hi or anything. He just stared. Three other employees came into the room, and the big wig ordered them to sit down on the end of the table next to me. I knew then I wasn't in here for the sales position. The employees around me were so nervous, they were making me nervous. I took out my little notebook and a pen, and I began to write.

NERVES
MONKEY BUSINESS

Eyes gazing into space
Lost in the Dipper's form,
Dilated from the Sun's cremation
And the supernova storm,
Searching high and low for something
But always falling short,
You had your tickets for the cruise,
But was left at the port.

They feed you plates and plates of lies
And you hunger for more
And know that hell's upset
Because I pimp the devil's whores,
Who smile and scheme of love and life
But only knows to hate
As they try to throw Molotov cocktails
Over Heaven's gates.

Brainchild born so prematurely
Now his brain is like a child's
But every time he looks at me
I see the angels smile.
And from that smile I form a star
And thrust it into the air,
So when you see a shooting star
Know that's my brainchild there.

I can see you're nervous
Like two strangers in the dark
Locked inside a room and standing
Just two feet apart,
They hold their breath and wonder
Just what's on the others' mind
Like a little monkey
Who don't know which tree to climb.

In ignorance we lose our innocence
To vicious fools
Who bait our insecurities
With things we thought were cool.
But only to discover it
Was just a worthless faze,
A dream we had so crystal clear
Now just a foggy haze.

Continue on your righteous path
But never hate the ones
That lost their way and now seeks guidance
From the drugs and guns,
I shot two missiles in the air
Two missiles that seek heat,
But the missiles only found each other
And brought their own defeat.

I said I pimp the devil's whores
I also rob his dealers.
I flush their product down the drain

To make room for natural healers,
I thought I saw the earthworm run,
The cheetah walks so slowly,
And God knows the heart of man
So quit acting like you holy.

I can see you're nervous
Like two strangers in the dark,
Locked inside a room and standing
Just two feet apart
They hold their breath and wonder
Just what's on the others' mind,
Like a little monkey
Who don't know which tree to climb.

SHOOK UP

Shook up,
They scared to look up
Staring at their shoes like they changing colors,
Rolls Royce dreams crashed into oblivion
Rolex can't keep up with the times,
Boys and girls switching teams like free agents
Still wondering were the playbook went,
As Encyclopedias suffer from amnesia
And the rainbow decided to just be gray,
Outlining a sorrowful sky
That overlooks a dreadful world.

Shook up,
They scared to look up,
Look up,
Look up…

Watching these "whatever wannabes"
Give these young girls goose bumps,
Falling in love with the thought or dream
Of being with a thug,
AKA an immature stuck nigga
You're just a Cadillac with no gas,
All looks and no drive,
And you really just flea market quality
Because half of y'all are fake,
Hiding behind mean-mugs
And Viacom-supplied fame.

Shook up,
They scared to look up,
Look up,
Look up,

Demons vacation in Antarctica,
Snow-sledding on Penguin's land
Cooling their lemonade with the iceberg
That sunk the Titanic,
And it's all paid for by the government,
Using money designated to urban society,
They say promises were made to broke,
So I retract my promise of peace
You don't know why dogs bark,
But you will know why you were bitten
And it has already begun
Because it was already written.

Shook up,
They scared to look up,
Shady businessmen wonder
Which delegate got the hook-up.
Rent out Hates Hotel until all the rooms took-up…

Look up,
Look up…

YESTERDAY (THE EXAMPLE) CONTINUED: LAID OFF

When the big wig walked back in the room, this is what he had to say:

Hello Sir or Ma'am,
Hope you are all doing fine,
I know you're all in suspense of why you're here,
So I won't take much time.
We liked you as an employee,
And we appreciate all the work you've done,
But we've decided to cut back in some areas,
And your area just happens to be one.
We didn't mean to shock you,
And I know you're wondering why,
And there's no easy way to say this,
But for y'all sake I'll try.
See,
You all have been here for years,
And have been doing excellent work,
But in order to pay you what you deserve,
That means our pockets will have to hurt,
And I know you're thinking,
"What does he mean, 'pockets will have to hurt?'
He's damn near a millionaire"
But we wear the 3-piece suits around here,
And that means we don't have to care,
We never listened to your suggestions,
Because you don't have a degree,
And without a piece of paper,

How could you be smarter than me?
And although you know this work better than I do,
I still think that you're dumb,
Because you're on a lower pay grade,
You'll never understand where I'm coming from,
And although you're good at your job,
We'll still release you with haste,
Because we'll fill half of your jobs with immigrants,
And the rest is just as easy to replace,
Due to the fact that,
Yes you're smart,
In all honesty probably smarter than me,
But I still think you're dumb,
You know why?
Because you'll never reach the place you'll need to be,
Yes you're full of potential,
But to me you're just a clown,
And every time you try to rise,
Either me,
Or your peer-pressuring friends,
Will hold you down…

Once again, I'd like to thank you
For working here,
Please clean out your area
And leave the premises,
Your final check will be in the mail.

    Those probably weren't his exact words, but that's basically what he said, hidden behind all the big words, economic excuses, and meaningless thank-yous.

PISSED OFF (EXPLICIT LYRICS PART II)

And here is me,
Swerving down 285 angrily
Pissed off at the world cuz the world is
Pissed off at me,
And I didn't do a damn thing to it,
That bullshit in Iraq? I didn't do it
Gas prices gone wack? I didn't do it
Fake war on crack? I didn't do it
Decide to be born black? I didn't do it...
Yet I cherish every moment of it,
From my athletic skills to my chocolate stare,
From my big dick to my nappy hair,
Yet still folk looking at me like, "How dare he?
He doesn't talk, dress or acts like me."
So I say fuck 'em
Cuz all they gonna do is try to fuck me.
Let boatloads of crack enter from foreign countries
Into our town,
Then when my hands touch it, I get 30 years locked down,
But when I tried to live with you,
You didn't want me around,
Yet your sons and daughters go out of their way
Trying to imitate our style,
And no I'm not a racist,
I'm just a realist
And any black person who was kicked out of their home
For so bullshit "Urban Renovation"
So you can relocate your peers

And do us like you did the Native Americans,
Sending them on a "trail of tears",
Any black person whose child went to Iraq
And didn't come back,
And the government said "he died of a heart attack"
Come to find out the truth was hid from the information wire
Your son was really killed by friendly fire
Cuz he and his commanding officer
Got into an argument cuz he called
Bush a fuckin' liar,
Any black person that's sick and tired,
All y'all gotta feel me.
And here is me,
Swerving down 285 angrily,
Until I realize Jesus was black like me,
And since I'm made in his image and likeness
When they diss me,
They're really dissing G.O.D.
Dang.

RETIRED NIGGER

So I see you've decided to retire the word NIGGER.

Clap Clap Clap

I'm so proud of you.

In fact,

I might just retire the word NIGGER too,

Hell it won't change a thing

You'll still be a nigger,

Selling my drugs and pulling my triggers,

And I know you think this is the time to stop saying nigger

Cuz it's time to take a stand against the brutality against niggers

But most of that brutality comes from other niggers

Who wasn't taught by the older niggers nothing

So instead of talking he'd rather pull my trigger,

And we ship his ass off to jail real quick

Because for every head in jail we make $$ figures $$,

And your nigger politicians go rally

To get other niggers released but hell,

It's a NIGGER that decided to keep Genarlow Wilson in jail,

Cuz niggers love to politic when there in a position of power,

Cuz we change they're mindset about the other niggers

Who only get paid by the hour,

They gotta play our game and if they go against me,

We'll do they ass like we did Cynthia McKinney.

See you and your politicians march and rally over a word,

When instead of concentrating on nouns

Y'all should concentrate on verbs,

Going out and being responsible

For the welfare of your community
Rather than retiring a word that's said
By YOU more than ME,
It don't matter if its NIGGA or NIGGER,
You won't catch us rallying
About you calling us cracker
And I know you think NIGGER
Was a form of oppression
But you're only oppressed now
Due to your own suppression,
We don't sell the dope,
We don't throw the trash,
We don't shoot the guns,
We don't waste the cash,
But we'll continue to HELP you do it,
We've been afraid of you for years,
But niggers won't rise above us cuz
Niggers are they're own worse fear.
Y'all retire a word
But haven't retired workplace prejudice,
Unfair neighborhood re-orgs and police stereotyping.
You haven't even retired gangs and drugs in your community!
PATHETIC NIGGER!
Go fight my war,
I'll make sure you return home cold,
That strike against Don Imus?
That was my amusement,
I don't mind putting a flunky on the bench,
You STILL take what I give you,
But for a word you'll throw a tantrum,

But I bet you'll still stand your ass up

For my national anthem!

Ignorant ass!

Ha ha ha

Why retire the word nigger?

You still a nigger,

Selling my drugs and pulling my triggers.

I'll just sit my cracker ass down

And watch some niggers coon on BET.

GOTTA GO

Reality is a very touchy-feely phenomenon. Sometimes it likes to take its time, and other times it seems to strike automatically. But, rest assured, sooner or later it will hit you. Sometimes reality is expected, other times it's a totally unexpected and emotional shock. It is during that time when you must decide how you plan on handling it. You can't sit in sorrow; you have to face your reality standing up. So, I've decided to do more than just stand and face it. I want to change it. How will I do that, though? I can't do it here. Not with my current state of mind. I must allow my mind to leave this place if I ever want to become anything fruitful in life. So, I gotta go. I gotta give my mind room to breathe. I feel as though something is suffocating me. I gotta get outta here. I gotta take my mind on a journey. Allow it to see new things, challenge itself, its palate, and even its own thought pattern. Where can I do this? I don't know. But I do know one thing for certain, and that's the fact that I gotta go.

TRAVELIN' MAN (RUNAWAY LETTER)

Dear Brother and Sister,

I'm travelin' man. I got nothing but the clothes on my back, the thoughts in my mind, the words in my mouth and the Good Book in my palm. I have no specific destination: any map or compass to lead the way. If I do find myself at a crossroads, I'll just have to kneel down and pray. I gotta go, man. I can't stay here. I tired of being surrounded by worried and fear. I put myself on the backburner just to help others rise, but when it was my turn to rise, well, let's just say I learned that you can't depend on no man to survive. This life I live ain't mines no more. It's his and hers'. I sat on street corners that I thought I owned. I hung out with folks that I thought was my friends. The streets weren't ever mine, and those weren't ever my friends. Even the chameleon will show his true colors in the end. So, I'm travelin' man. Why is everyone here happy with failure? Why is everyone comfortable with defeat? Why is it that, when I try to better myself for my future and my family, these young niggas start hating almost immediately? When will these people stop sleepwalking and wake up to reality? They gotta see. Man, they gotta see. I guess the Land of the Sleepwalkers just isn't the land for me. So I'm travelin' man. My destination is unknown. But I know that I can't stay here surrounded by thieves and clones. Surrounded by lies and failure, and those afraid of the truth to the point were they'd die over something that depreciates rather than live for something that's eternal. I'll send word once I reach my destination.

Peace.

Brainstorm

I want,

I need,

I must succeed

Go there,

Get that,

Flip that,

Get more,

Go back,

Get that,

Recycle the process

No more knocking,

I must kick in doors

Been there,

Seen more,

Seen glory,

Seen gore

Had women,

Had whores,

Good fellas,

Bad boys

He pissed with a bad toy,

He put you off in a bag boy,

You can't dodge the system,

You here better be glad boy,

Make yourself into somebody

They claim to have so much joy

Now they all say they knew you

Before you became McCoy,

Label me crazy,
But she saw your Mercedes
And you fell for that game,
And she spitting out babies,
Now she just like that baby,
Depending on you it's crazy
But ain't nothing to say
Cuz we made it that way,
Now child support hound you,
They say you a scoundrel,
While she buy that D & B purse,
She steady clown you
Authentic and all true,
Situation is all you,
Complicated by all rules
Made by politic fools,
It's a situation chosen
When we refuse to choose,
I might be down a touchdown
But still I refuse to lose.
Some friends came,
Now they gone,
Shared a house,
Now no one's home,
Off in sin,
Then again,
Where were we to begin?
M.I.A. when we lose,
In your face when we win
Life done dealt a heavy blow,

And we took it on the chin…

My Brainstorm,

Squeezed thru the eye of a needle

Swam thru the eye of the storm with no harm

This my Brainstorm,

Slept in the Jezebel dorm,

Saw straight thru Lucifer's charm

Remain strong

And have a Brainstorm…

A RAMBLE FORMED IN THE LOST SIDE OF THE BRAIN (NO WAY HOME)

Why do we keep thinking that
We got it together,
Like our brain cells are just fine,
But we use only 10 percent,
It know something's up because it
Feel like my soul is paying rent,
For living on Earth,
Niggas struggling since birth
For a meal plan,
Wealthy man won't lend a hand,
So I'm going broke trying to make more dough,
Wearing my hat with the brim low
And I feel for,
Them children living off that stem growth
Or on cooked white sky,
Staring into Daddy's blood shot eyes,
Mama stuck her body up,
Too high to cry,
Can't figure this out with my natural mind,
They're waiting for tomorrow but these are the end times.
Enquiring minds wonder but insightful minds stay silent,
If you're life is like a sitcom,
Who's writing the pilot?
Got to seek knowledge but we still finding violence,
No lessons are taught cuz dead mouths stay silent,

Niggas busy wilding but yet we say we vibing,

We're just lying,

We laying face down on the ground

With a canine in the back seat

Sniffing the pound,

Them blue lights vibrate off your kids face,

The disappointment shown...

Lost on these streets with NO WAY HOME,

Thought you in the clear,

We done cried too much why shed a tear,

People start to thinking,

"This world corrupt,

So why am I legal?

Working got me Marta,

But trapping got me Regal",

We in this world by fate,

Of it by choice,

Listening to hell's yells drowning out God's voice,

You say you aim high,

So why are you all on my toes?

Success thru imperfect trails

Makes for immaculate foes,

Sure as the wind blow,

If they have rules,

Then watch us bend more,

You into dough,

But no recipe has got your bread low,

So we bend more

Till we break in two,

Ain't much a chiropractor can do,

When that evil pixie on your shoulder
Gets the best of you,
"They chopped down my oxygen no more shade,
Don't wanna be the one working for slave wages
Thinking I'm paid"…
The odor they smelled,
They found a 15-year old
Girl strangled and raped,
She was just making sure the lights stayed on
One minute,
The next minute she's gone,
Lost in reality with NO WAY HOME,
Like Stephen we stoned,
Immature mind but body grown,
Together we'd have stayed strong,
But stingy kids don't share,
Race of life like the tortoise and the hare
We didn't pace ourselves,
Microwave generation doing just fine…
Take your time,
Let it marinate sometimes.
Young and old pay attention,
It ain't the dessert,
It's the meat of the earth that's essential,
Use God's word as your war utensils
Unlimited ammo,
Keep the beam on their forehead,
Cuz if it wasn't for truth they'll be more dead,
Like David battling Goliath with no stones
No sling shot,

Before the fight even starts,
He's got.
Yet the plot thickens,
Cuz niggas don't know what the dickens
They here for,
No dreams or purpose,
So they stay in the slums smoking and snorting,
They don't understand
That we all one,
We are just from different mommas,
If there's no you there's no me,
Without the curve there's no comma,
The hate imploded on society some can't stomach
In this crab generation
Pulling each other down,
Loved ones even begin hating
Their souls are doing dirty dances with Satan,
Planet turned sideways,
There's no one left to trust nowadays,
Damn,
But the way many see it is,
"If everyday is a holiday
I guess crime gotta pay
Eventually,
Right?"
It's time you changed your tone
Before you become,
Lost in reality with NO WAY HOME.

GETTING GONE (TRAVELIN' SONG)

I'm traveling down this narrow road,
With a pain all in my soul,
I got to find a better way,
Or I won't make it thru the day,
My feet may hurt,
My legs getting weary,
But my heart must remain strong,
I'm Getting Gone
Getting Gone
Getting Gone,

They say there's a light at the end of the tunnel,
But all I see is dark and gloom,
I pray to God that they're right,
Because I may get tired soon,
My feet may hurt,
My legs getting weary,
But my heart must remain strong,
I'm Getting Gone
Getting Gone
Getting Gone,

You may ask me where I'm going,
Sad thing is I don't know myself,
All I know is I can't stay here,
Because it'll take me to my death,
My feet may hurt,
My legs getting weary,
But my heart must remain strong,

I'm Getting Gone
Getting Gone,
I'm Getting Gone.

I'm travelin', man. I'm on the road with no specific destination, but I'll know I've arrived when I get there. Or at least I hope I will.

VACANCY (BASS HEAD)

I needed a place to stay for the night. I looked around for shelter but I saw nothing in sight. Where I was at, everyone's shelter seemed to be underneath bridges or on the steps of churches. I walked and walked, hoping to see a hotel or someone I knew that would let me spend the night. It wasn't looking too good for me. I was just about to find a nice bench to lay on when I saw a small sign flickering from across the street. I walked over to it. The sign read "vacancy" in very dull, neon red letters. The steel-gated door underneath it was rusty and most of the windows where boarded, so I thought that the place was closed. But the light drizzle of rain was starting to pick-up, so I said a short prayer under my breath, and gave the doorknob a twist. It was unlocked.

As the heavy door creaked open, I slowly peeked inside. In the dimly lit room, I saw a dusty, old living room set, and rusted metal folding chairs against the pale wall. Above the chairs there was a sign that read *Heavenly Estates* in bold cursive writing.

"More like *Hell's Estates*," I chuckled to myself. I stepped into the building, and saw a receptionist counter near a thin hallway in the corner. I looked for an attendant but saw no one. I walked over to the counter and rang the bell, but no one came.

"Hello!" I yelled. No answer. As I let out a sigh, I could feel someone's breath brush across my neck. I turned around.

"What you want, boy?" boomed a deep-voiced man.

"Ah!" I screamed. "Why you come up behind me like that?"

"You scared?" he quipped.

"Nah man, you just-"

"What you want, boy?" he interrupted. I thought about just leaving, but the sound of rain hitting the pavement outside changed my mind.

"Do y'all have a room?" I asked.

"Don't the sign outside read 'vacancy'?" he quipped. "Look, you can't be leaving no pipes or razorblades in the room, and its $35 a night. If you got one of them prostitutes with you from outside, it's $50. Don't lie, cuz I know all of them, and Pimpin' Lee and me ain't cool no more." I was puzzled and offended at the same time.

"Man, I don't have any drugs or whores with me!" I snarled. He gave me a strange look, as if what I said puzzled him.

"What are you doing here, then?" he asked.

"I'm traveling thru, and I missed the last bus. I just need a room for tonight."

The man walked around me and to the counter, and pulled out a pack of chewing tobacco from his pocket, and stuffed it in his cheek.

"I apologize, but I don't get many customers like you anymore," he said as he spit out the tobacco juice into an empty Coke can. "Most folk come here either to get high or to get head." I kind of figured that before he said anything, and for that reason I really didn't want to pay $35 to stay here, even if it was cheap. I had to talk him down.

"I really wasn't expecting to be stuck on this side of town," I said in a sad, lowly voice. "I was trying to find a temp agency and got lost. All I got on me is $25." I held my head down low, hoping for some sympathy.

The man spat in his can and started laughing. "That's the best you can do? Ha! Honestly, that was the best acting I done seen all day. A crackhead stole my portable TV last night, and I've needed something to take my mind off this place. They gonna shut this place down soon, man. Yeah, give me $25. I'll use that to buy me a new portable TV." He reached under the desk and pulled out a key that read 2A.

"Upstairs, second door on the right," he said. I walked thru the thin hallway and up the stairs. The floor was sticky, and the hall smelled of urine and alcohol. I went inside my room to find there wasn't much change inside. A coffee table with cigarette butts in the ashtray, a TV that was bolted to the dresser, and a disgusting toilet with a cracked mirror and a rusted sink greeted me as I walked around the room.

I didn't even bother to look at the shower. The bed was big, and the sheets didn't look half bad, but I wasn't going to sleep inside the sheets tonight. I even kept my shoes on. At least my window wasn't boarded. One thing I really liked about the room was the big metal ceiling fan in the middle of the ceiling. I lay back on the bed and stared up at the ceiling fan. As I tried to relax, a beat began to play in my mind. It was Cee-Lo Green's *Bass Head Jazz.* My head began to rock back and forth as the horns blared in my head, and the spin of the ceiling fan mixed with the light tapping of rain I could hear on my window pane made my mind leave the smelly hotel and enter a whole different realm. All of a sudden, my mouth began to move...

"I'm searching,
With a flashlight in an urban fortress,
Got me asking myself,
Is it really worth it?
Came in with an eagerness
But what's the purpose?
I see the liquor store,
It's right next to where the church is.
So I'm a stop sinning,
But let me take a sip first,
This makes you feel like
All your feelings are worthless,
Bought a keg of lies from where
The evil ones lurk,
Now I want a refund
But forgot my proof of purchase,
So what do I do?
I guess I just sip the brew,
Swallow it slow and you can sip it too.

Pour some out for a my niggas who,
Instead of seeing the truth,
Saw the lies and went and fell for it too,
So yeah I got problems just like you,
When I shower I wish sometimes
The pain could go down that drain too.
But it's not anything that I can't handle,
When the ground's too hot I gotta put on sandals,
I just gotta know,
What's the purpose?
I'm travelin' man,
Left behind the swears but I brought along curses,
The ones that are emphasized in between verses,
The ones the lady screams when they out snatching purses,
The ones the guys scream when their friends are in hearses,
The ones your mind screams when
You don't know what your worth is.
So I'm still hoping that this too shall pass,
So I lay staring at the ceiling fan to
Bass Head Jazz,
If I could play life like this horn
Then it wouldn't be so bad,
Until then I lay listening to
Bass Head Jazz,
If I could…"

Bam! Bam! Bam! A heavy knock on the wall interrupts my flow.
"Eh, cut all that noise out," a man yells, "you're messing up my high." I curled over on my side and close my eyes.
"If only he could hear the beat in my mind," I thought to myself, and went to sleep.

DREAMS (IN TECHNICOLOR)

Dreaming in color,
I used to close my eyes and see gray skies,
Black clouds dripping sorrowful pale tears,
Fire red flames burning against my soul,
White ashes would flicker into thin air,
But soon the rain would fall harder,
Drenching the fire away
As smoke rose from the ground thick and opaque,
Then a bright yellow light peaked
From behind tall, brown trees with dark green leaves,
The light mixed with the dark clouds,
Making lavender lines in the sky
Until the sun,
Big and orange surrounded by swirls of red,
Rose deep in the East,
And all of a sudden,
The sky became so clear,
And a rainbow shot across the sky like a silver star,
The yellow and blue flowers began to bloom,
Beautiful white lilies sprung from the dogwoods,
And violets peaked from behind the weeds,
The dilapidated wood became strong in structure,
The dark, rotted spots became a strong chocolate display,
Red and white roses mixed with green baby's breath
Creating an awe-inspiring display,
Dreaming in color,
No more is my dreams all gray,

I see beauty when I sleep,

So I awake expecting a beautiful day.

NO CONTINENTAL BREAKFAST

I was awaken the next day by a bunch of yelling and swears coming from the hallway. I let out a huge yawn and rolled my way out of the bed and into the bathroom. I turned on the sink and splashed some water into my face, and then I stared at myself in the mirror. I was still a little perturbed about my thought process being interrupted yesterday. It's very frustrating to have a natural high blown due to an artificial one.

"One day," I thought to myself, "My mind will be respected." I quickly gathered myself together and headed downstairs. Looking at the lobby in the daytime, I could tell that this place used to be beautiful. I guess it's true that, when a little love is forgotten, it can turn anything from precious to rotten. I headed to the counter to drop off my key, but I didn't see anyone. So I sat the key down on the counter, and, as I was about to turn to exit, I felt heavy breathing against my neck.

"What you want, boy?" boomed a deep-voiced man. I circled around quickly. It was the owner, once again creeping up on me.

"You sure like to come up behind people, don't you?" I quipped.

"Aw nigga, quick being so sensitive," he replied. "So, did you sleep well?" Before I could answer, he interrupted, "You ain't gotta lie. I know that was probably the worst sleep you ever had in your life. Now look, ain't no continental breakfast. If you drink coffee, I got some in the pot over there. It ain't decaf, though. It's real strong; it'll wake you up." I walked over to the pot and poured some coffee into a paper cup.

"Thanks," I said. "Do you mind if I asked you a question? What happened to this place?"

He laughed. "Reality happened. Shit, don't nothing last forever. Yeah, this place used to be something, but now it's nothing. It was *Heavenly Estates*, a place to relax. Now it's *Heavenly Estates*, a place to get high. It's going to close soon, anyway. Even the finest, biggest-booty supermodel you've ever seen will one day shrivel up like a prune and die. That's life, nigga." After he said that, he turned and walked off, shoving a handful of chewing tobacco into his jaw. I just shook my head, stepped out the door, and walked outside the hotel. I noticed it had stopped raining. I walked across the street and over to a nearby bench. I turned around, and looked at the hotel. The reason that the hotel was in such bad condition had nothing to do with the town. It had everything to do with the townspeople's attitude. If the attitude is, "fuck it, it's gonna die anyway", then what's the purpose of ever loving it to begin with? With a name like *Heavenly Estates*, it should make me think of the comforts of Heaven, not the brimstone of Hell. I just stood there and stared at the hotel. I thought about all the potential that place had, and wondered what it could look like if someone just loved it enough to believe in it, take care of it, and help nurture it. I went to take a sip of the coffee.

"Dang," I said to myself, "the coffee has gotten cold."

COLD COFFEE

A cup of cold coffee,
Hope the coffee ain't too weak,
I need something to wake me up,
From this loathsome sleep.
So drowsy my eyes,
I can't keep them wide,
I can just barely see,
The reality that stands
Right in front of me.
When I go to touch it,
I miss a step and nearly fall,
Almost dropping my coffee and all,
And when I try to talk,
And say what's on my mind
When I open my mouth
All I do is
YYYAAAWWWNNN…..
Dang, excuse me.
What was I saying?
I must still be halfway asleep,
I can't remember what's on my mind,
And if I'm in a state like this,
How could I know if everything's fine?
I'm so vulnerable to lies,
So wide-open to failure,
So close to just falling down,
So much like many people in this town…
We're just sleepwalking.

Just waiting for the weekend,

Hoping that today will just end

So that I could just leave this God-forsaking job,

Then when I get home I just wanna leave these God-forsaking kids,

I fill my mind, my body, and my soul with defecate foolishness,

Then I say, "I'm so tired of this shit."

But I've been talking it all day,

I've carried that expression on my face,

Just that you wouldn't wanna talk to me,

And when people came around to wake me up,

I'd snap on them and yell,

"LEAVE ME ALONE! JUST LET ME SLEEP!"

But I'm too tired to keep being tired,

This sleepwalking has drained my soul,

Just lying rolled up in sorrow has made me weary,

And my current state has gotten old.

I'm ready to wake up.

A cup of cold coffee,

Hope the coffee ain't too weak,

I need something to wake me up,

From this loathsome sleep.

Another Brainstorm

Old School,
New School,
Old job,
New cash,
More money,
More taxes,
More lips on your ass,
More chains,
More whips,
New slaves,
Old rules,
More died,
More jailed,
More scared,
Old news,
Never played your cards
He folds,
You fold too,
Never looked in the mirror,
Met someone who knows you
When to church Sunday,
What the preacher said so true,
Walked out of church Sunday,
Ran into the old you,
Caught up on old times,
Ran into some old friends
Caught up on old dirt,
Ran into that mess again,

Not satisfied,
So you fake and flex again,
Deceit packed in your heart
Smothering your innocence,
More greed,
More war,
But we re-elect again,
Train them,
Teach them,
Hell,
Even shake they hand,
Pay me upfront,
And I'll let them in,
And look somber
In front of cameras for children,
No Malcolm,
No Pac,
No Martin,
No Smalls,
No leaders,
No stance,
No words,
No cause.
Niggas talk real big,
But really,
No balls,
Niggas' speech got claps,
But really,
No applause,
Niggas' turned their back

I can't be more appalled,
Niggas on the wrong track,
Scared to be more involved
Niggas say they want out
But to death they installed,
Niggas stuck in poverty
Claiming that they ball…

My Brainstorm,
Squeezed thru the eye of a needle
Swam thru the eye the storm with no harm
This my Brainstorm,
Slept in the Jezebel dorm,
Saw straight thru Lucifer's charm
Remain strong
And have a Brainstorm…

MR. G-MAN

I found myself sitting on a hard concrete slab under the streetlight with my paper and pen in my hands, and a cold cup of coffee beside me. I looked out on the town and didn't see anything worth drawing. It's just the same old folks on the same old corners doing the same old thing. The dilapidated wood on the side of the houses were a pale green, and the looks on its occupants faces were a pale blue. The liquor store and mom and pop store has been hidden the shadows of the new high-rises, and the old apartments were torn down, leaving a flattened dirt path with a huge yellow digger in the middle of the lot. I guess there's a transformation going on in this town. Yet, as I looked out upon it sitting on the concrete slab, I saw nothing new. It's just the same old folks on the same old corners doing the same old thing.

Some of the people that used to live here were forced to move by the Rehabilitation Project this city is enforcing. The funny thing about that is I never see anyone who was forced to leave move back into the "rehabilitated" land. And no one that's not from this area wants to move over here due to its unfortunate reputation. So, now I see more cops on the street arresting homeless people who are just trying to get something to eat. I see the price tag on everything skyrocketing out of control, and I see businesses lying off workers that had been with the company for so long that's all that they knew. There's no severance pay to account for that. So now the oppression that was once over this town that this new Rehabilitation Project is supposed to fix has succumbed to acceptance. Everyone around here is comfortable being the same old folks sitting on the same old corners doing the same old thing. Damn.

I came up with a plan. From where I sat, I could vaguely see the big city nightlights and skyscrapers thru the foggy night sky. I decided that I would draw the big city skyline, following the main road that leads to where I sat. I would also draw the buildings across the street from me, and I would put a rainbow across the sky as a symbolism of hope for the now and the future. As I rested the paper across my thigh and began to put ink to it, I heard a noise from across the street. On the side of a green garbage disposal lie a man, convulsing on the ground and shivering in his own vomit. The people that were with him looked at him with a nonchalant stare: as if what they were witnessing was the norm.

"Oh, shit! G-Man, are you alright?" one asked.

"Hey, G-Man, get up," another demanded. He stopped shaking.

"Ah, he's fucked up," another one said, coming to a sad realization. "Let's get outta here." As the others scurried off leaving the man, I got up and walked towards him. The closer I got to him, the more I could smell the loud stench of defecation and vomit. I looked into his eyes. His eyes were bugged white with a frightened stare. On his arm was a tattoo that read "G-Man". Right above the tattoo there was a needle in his arm. I walked back across the street and drank the last sip of cold coffee, then walked back across the street and threw the cup away in the dumpster near the deceased. I was no longer in the mood to draw. How can I find beauty when all I see is ugliness? I went into the adjacent store and walked up to the counter.

"Gimme a $1 scratch-off," I said. "Oh, by the way, y'all might wanna call the police. Someone just OD'd by the dumpster."

The cashier frowned angrily. "Not again! Damn!" I just shook my head, took my ticket, and walked away.

I grabbed my key, said a little prayer, and scratched off my ticket. I didn't win. I was about to throw it away when I thought of the dead man again. I turned my ticket over, grabbed my ticket and wrote a little song for him.

Mr. G-Man,

I didn't know you until I saw you in the street,

Eyes bugged and heart without a beat.

What did the G stand for?

It could've been for George

Like George Washington Carver,
But I guess your life was harder.
You probably won't make the front page news,
But will be a good verse for singing the blues,
Mr. G-Man.

HUSTLING: PART ONE

      Sitting at the bus stop waiting on the bus to arrive, a funny site caught my eyes. Near the trash can, behind a raggedy fold-away table, on two empty milk crates sat a man. With a small red ball and three thistles he captivated the attention of a small crowd. He moved the thistles in his hands swiftly around the table, and then he came to a sudden stop.

      "Where is it?" he asked. A man wearing a tight button-down shirt with a Gheri curl walked forward and pointed at a thistle.

      "The one on the right", the man replied. The man behind the table lifted the thistle, revealing the small red ball.

      "Dang, you won!" he exclaimed as he dug in his pocket and handed the man some cash. The Gheri-curled man took the money with a big smile, and stepped to the side.

      "Anybody else wanna play?" the other man asked. For a moment, no one responded. After a while, a young girl emerged from the back of the crowd holding an envelope in her hand.

      "I'll play," she said in a low voice. The man smiled.

      "Alright," he said, as he set the thistles in a row. "How much are you willing to bet?" The young girl looked into the envelope and pulled out a $50 bill. The man's smile grew from ear to ear.

      "Fifty it is," he said. "Watch the ball." The man put the red ball underneath the middle thistle, then begun to switch the thistles around. He swiftly moved his hands around and around, then stopped.

      "Okay, where is it?" The girl pointed confidently at the middle thistle.

      "That one right there," she said. The man lifted the thistle, and, sure enough, there was the small red ball.

      "Damn!" he man cursed angrily as he dug into the back pocket and gave her a torn $50 bill. He looked over at the guy with the curl, and shook his head.

"Good job, sweetheart. Try it again though." The girl thought about it for a second.

"No, that's alright, I'm done," she said.

"Aw, c'mon, we'll make it double or nothing," the man replied. "You got me once, you might get me again." Feeling confident, the girl agreed to play again. The man's smile was nearly off his face now. I walked over closely so that I may see the game from a better view. Once again, the man moved the thistles swiftly, back and forth, around and around, before coming to an abrupt stop with all the thistles in a perfect row.

"Where is it," he asked again. The girl, once again, confidently pointed at the thistle, this time at the one on the left.

"That one right there," she said. The man grabbed the left thistle, slightly moving it. A sly grin went across the face of the curly-haired man. It was obvious to me what just transpired. The man on the milk crates lifted the thistle. Nothing was there.

"You lose, baby," the man said, sticking out his hand for payment. The girl slowly dug into her envelope and pulled out $100 and gave it to the man. As the men went along with their game, the girl eyes began to wail up as the walked pass me. She looked so hurt and innocent, it kind of touched my heart, and I couldn't let them get away with it. As she tried to walk pass, I grabbed the girl by her arm, startling her.

"I didn't mean to scare you, but hold on one second." I pulled her over to the table and interrupted the game.

"Hustle me like you just hustled her," I snarled at the man sitting down. Before he could even respond his juicy-haired friend leaped into my face. He started mean-mugging and showing off his fake gold teeth.

"Eh man, we over here trying to play a game and you trying to mess up my money!" he yelled. He stepped closer, so I sized him up, not backing down at all.

"If you ain't in cahoots with this man, then you shouldn't mind me taking his money. So step back." The man looked over at his friend, and the man nodded.

"It's okay," he said, "if the man wants to play, let him play. How much you want to lose?" I looked over at the girl, who was in awe at what I was doing, and I pulled out my money.

"Two hundred," I said. The crowd let out a collective gasp. He looked over at his friend, as if he didn't have enough money on him.

"Go ahead and get some money from him if you're short," I snapped. The man seemed to get upset.

"Quit worrying about him, I got this, nigga!" he growled, slamming the thistles down in the table. "Watch the damn ball!" The man put the red ball under the middle thistle and began to swirl his hands around frantically, going faster and faster, much faster than before when the young girl was playing. I kept my eyes close on the thistle the entire time, watching its every move. Finally, he came to a stop. It was WAY too easy. That's the problem with poor hustlers, they half-do everything.

"With just your index and thumb, pick up the right one," I said sternly. Don't hit the table or shake the thistle. If you do I'm taking all your money."

"Nigga, don't tell me what to do!" he shouted. His facial expression said it all. He picked up the thistle. There lay the red ball. Obviously, he didn't take the loss well.

"Fuck this! Game Over!" he yelled, quickly grabbing his game pieces and flipping the table over, nearly hitting several bystanders.

"That's fine if you want to end the game, but you need to pay up," I said. As I said that, the Gheri-curled man walked up behind, screaming illegibly. The crowd started dispersing, and I could see the bus coming from up the hill. I bumped hard into the man purposely, and he pushed me off and took a swing at me, but he missed. I handed the girl my bus card.

"Here," I said, "get on the bus." As the crowd dispersed and the bus got to its stop, I looked back at the two hustlers who were turning the corner. One looked back at me and mouthed something I couldn't make out. I just laughed at them.

HUSTLING: PART TWO

I got on the bus with the young girl. She used my card and I paid cash, and we sat near the back. She slouched in her seat with a very disappointed look on her face.

"Are you alright?" I asked.

"I was just trying to get some extra money", she said solemnly, handing me back my bus card. "Thank you for trying to get it back for me. I don't know what I'm going to do." She peaked back into her envelope, counted her remaining money and started to cry. "My first dang paycheck! A hundred of it is gone already."

"Actually, it's just fifty he got from you," I said, correcting her. "It could've been worse. Why were you trying to gamble with them anyway?" She looked up at me.

"You just don't understand," she sobbed.

"I might understand more than you think," I replied. She folded her envelope and put it in her pocket. Wiping the tears from her eyes, she began to explain:

Ain't a pretty day for me,
Even when the sun is out,
Everyday is cloudy for me,
Even in the summer rain,
Everyday's a drought for me.
I've been hustling all my life,
My daddy died when I was three,
And my mama became an alcoholic,
So no one was there to raise me but me,
Grandma too old to chase me,
Aunts and uncles didn't care to face me,

So I'm out there on these streets,
Just trying to get something to eat,
Just trying to keep lights on cuz mama,
She's battling her own beasts.
So I've been working hard my whole life,
Just trying to make things right.
Hustling everyday,
I'm tired of damn hustling
I just want to go away!
I just want a vacation,
I just want to be able to live
Carefree but I can't cuz everything I get
I have to give.
See this envelope?
I started a new job two weeks ago,
And in this was my first paycheck,
But I knew this money would be gone
On overdue bills and I was thinking,
"Dang I've spent this and I haven't even
Cashed it in yet"
But this isn't anything new,
In fact it's getting quite old.
Living check to check and still coming up short
Like last week I had to pond all my daddy's gold,
His gold chain and his gold watch,
And that's all I had left of him,
But I had to do it just to keep the lights from going dim.
When I was with my mama we got evicted twice,
So there was times where I slept with men
Just to spend the night,

And so eventually I got money from these men,
And used that to help pay the bills,
But the bills kept stacking up,
And my mama kept saying she was too ill
To go back to work,
But I was ill too!
I've had three abortions,
Three!!
And it's been the grace of God I haven't
Caught a terminal STD,
And my mama knew this so I realized
She didn't care about me,
So I left with a man who constantly beat me,
And finally he beat me to the point
Where I couldn't even see,
And I knew that this place wasn't the place for me,
But if he had never got arrested for drug trafficking
I'd still be there today,
If he hadn't already killed me,
Bad news is now I once again had no money,
So I moved back in with my mama
Because for a while I had no j-o-b,
You see I dropped out of school when I was 13,
And I haven't had time to get my G.E.D.
Until about a month ago,
I was riding the 83,
And this chick sat on the row next to me,
Left her book bag on the bus accidentally,
So I looked inside of it and saw her state I.D.,
And I'd be damned if in that picture,

She didn't look exactly like me.
Plus she had a wallet-sized copy of her diploma
In it too,
And I needed a job so what was I to do?
I used her identification and got myself some work.
And the money in this check was going to pay the rent,
And that's why I said this check was already spent,
And I just turned 18 not too long ago so I was gonna
See if I could get some money
To buy some new shoes
I haven't had any in about a year or two
And I was-

"Wait, wait, wait," I interrupted. You're eighteen and you've been thru all that?

"Unfortunately," she responded. I reached into my back pocket and pulled out a wallet. I looked inside of it, and it had about $400 in it.

"This belongs to that fake hustler," I said, tossing her the wallet. "Happy belated birthday." She opened the wallet and took out the money as a smile swept across her face. "Sometimes life can seem so unfair," I said, "but if you stay in the game eventually you'll win. I've been needing a vacation, too. Although I can't afford to actually go anywhere, I'm travelin', sister. You can travel with me if you want."

"Thank you so much," she exclaimed. "I have to get some things taken care of, but one day I might take you up on that. By the way, what's your name?"

"Jay, what's yours?"

"Sunshine."

"That's a pretty name." She blushed.

"Thank you. Maybe one day I'll live up to it."

SUNSHINE

I see a beautiful creation,
One of God's masterpieces,
A breathtaking vision like she could be
One of Heaven's nieces,
A sublime array of texture handcrafted by the Jehovah,
With eyes that burst with color like a golden supernova,
She can cause a heart attack when she blinks her eyes,
Respiratory problems when she steps,
So wonderful that when God carved her he had to say
"Well done" to himself,
Natural beauty beyond the mountains
With lips that makes more honey than bees,
With lavender-scented hair,
And a smile you wouldn't believe…
But the sad thing is that neither does she believe,
Because although she is beautiful,
She has yet to just
Be.
And she was put on this Earth to shine,
Even when the day has its dawn,
But right now she doesn't see herself as a queen,
Because she feels she's been playing the pawn.
I just wish she could see what I see,
She was named Sunshine for a reason,
The sun will shine on us
No matter the season,
And she's supposed to shine on the world,
But it's hard to shine when you're not believing.

Maybe she just needs to get away,
Even the sun sets until another day,
And I know it's hard to get away
When rent's due and bills have to be paid,
But maybe her mind could hang out with the stars,
Let Jupiter take her to a show,
Or listen to Mars play his saxophone,
So that when she returns she can show the world
Her natural glow,
Or maybe she just needs to go,
Start travelin' like me for a time,
Because everyone on Earth has to have
A little Sunshine.
I see a beautiful creation,
One of God's masterpieces,
A breathtaking vision like she could be
One of Heaven's nieces…
I just wish she could see it too.

YOU'RE BEAUTIFUL (A SONG FOR YOU)

I know you had a tough day
But I want to make everything ok.
Your bath water was already run.
You step in slowly,
As lavender bubbles tickle your skin,
The candlelight flickers
And the champagne warms you from within,
I stare into your eyes and say,
You're beautiful....
Let me just touch you,
Let me message your stress away,
Let me rub your feet,
Cuz you've been running thru my mind all day,
Let me kiss your feet,
Chills run up thru you and make your weak,
I just look at you to speak,
You're beautiful...
Let me give you a natural high,
Let me kiss you on your thigh,
Let my hands explore your skin,
From your navel to your chin,
Let me kiss your lips and say,
You're beautiful...
Let me carry your soaking skin to the bed,
Let me kiss you on your neck,
Let me kiss you on your back,

From your shoulders to your crack,
Let me my hands massage away your pain,
Let my tongue relieve your strain,
Let me make your whole body scream,
Make your cum flow like a stream...
I want to make it all okay.
Let me take that burden away,
So when the whole world treats you ugly,
Just remember baby,
Your Beautiful....

THE ISLE OF A THOUSAND SMILES

She had her bags packed and everything.
She'd been planning this trip for years,
Her walking down with her eyes full of tears,
Cameras flashing,
Treating her like a star,
Her family and friends came to join her from afar.
She was ready to go to
The Isle of A Thousand Smiles…
She was so ready,
She'd been reading books and magazines,
Picking out garments and gowns,
Jewelry and food and a bunch of unnecessary things,
Her girlfriends had all gone before her,
They smile so big and seem so happy,
And she finally met a man willing to take her there,
Before even getting to know him she said,
Gladly,
She was ready to go to
The Isle of A Thousand Smiles…
And now she tells all of her friends,
Showing off the glistening rock on her hand,
They all smile and cheer for her so!
And she seems so happy that she has
Let all of her fears, inhibitions, and unfortunately,
Her common sense go,
So when he doesn't do right she ignores it,
He yells and screams and she adores it,
The Ying and Yang has never been so out of whack

But she continues to try and force them to match
Because in her mind nothing,
And I mean nothing,
Is going to ruin her trip to
The Isle of A Thousand Smiles…
And now her special day has come,
Her gown flows behind her so,
Cameras flashing and people cheering,
Flocking to her wherever she goes,
She loves every minute of it,
From his meaningless words
To the meaningless kiss,
And her dream of going to the isle has come true,
Sending her mind into a beautiful bliss,
But the trip wouldn't be as beautiful as she dreamed.
There was false advertisement all over that brochure,
Screams during the day and silence during the night,
When they wasn't having sex all they did was fight,
It rained and rained repeatedly on her window pane
Until it got to the point when her stomach curled
When she would lie beside him at night…
This was a nightmare.
Everything she had hoped for and dreamed,
Crashed into reality,
She wished so much that she could get a refund
And just go home,
For she realized that the trip she so longed for was
Not the trip she should've rushed into all along,
And if she had saw the signs before the reservations were made,
She could've left him alone,

And found the right man to take her
Into a beautiful place,
But she was in such a rush to visit
The Isle of A Thousand Smiles.

SUCTION

I'm stuck to the suction cup that is you,
Engulfing my soul like a tidal wave of glue,
Charlotte's web and I'm the fly,
Struggling for freedom but I can't move,
I've been trying to free myself for so long,
That I've nearly given up all hope.
When will you come finish me off?
When will you suck my soul dry?
I've grown weary of being here,
So now I just wonder,
When will I die?
I'm stuck to the suction cup that is you,
Paralyzed by your powerful grip,
Wondering how did I allow myself to slip
And fall this awfulness,
Ropes of destruction tied into a knot,
So tight it cuts off my self-esteem,
Struggling only makes the knot worse,
So now I'm too tired to dream,
So now I'm too tired to scream,
I want someone to rescue me,
Take me away from everything
Because I'm not as happy as I may seem,
Stuck in this web with an evil thing,
Named You…
I'm stuck to the suction cup that is you,
I need to escape but I'm afraid to,
So now instead of living my life,

I just lie here tied up next to you….

Please,

Either finish me off or let me be free!

RAMBLIN' WITH AN OLD SOUL

      I got off the bus at the train station, but I couldn't decide on which train I wanted to get on, so I just sat down on the bench, right next to an old man. There were some kids standing in front of us, having a freestyle cipher. They were rapping about girls and diamonds, Benzes they supposedly drive and crack they supposedly sold. Now, they were coming up with some nifty punch lines, but in my opinion, they weren't saying anything. But I listened closely, hoping to hear an intelligent line or two. Maybe one of them would even say a line that was actually a true account of something they've done or accomplished. It never happened. I don't know what took over me, but, all of a sudden I jumped up off of the bench and joined in:

I was invited to the party but I lost my invitation
So I crashed it like Bush did Saddam's dictation
As everybody there showed off their newest innovation
I used verbal illustration, I called it God's Creation
Planted rap seeds into beats, I'm in the waiting room pacing
She gave birth to a reFUGEE flow, I guess my son's Haitian
Now I'm trying for 2nd child, but what's my motivation
Should I rap for the soul or for standing ovations?
To please a suit or for spiritual elation?
Could I mix the 2 without getting bad vibrations?
See, he too cool for school but he not credible,
Yet we feed off of it and whatever else that's edible,
I saw the signs but the writings on the wall are no longer legible
Now rap is brain-dead, body just a vegetable.
I got the remedy but they say it cost too much,
It's hard to pay the price when you living a selfish life
So now rap ain't cool unless its full of strife,
Or hoes or clothes you ain't never bought in your life

Or cars you ain't never drove in your life
But you be keeping it real right?
Right....you a faker, get a life.

    When I was done, the other guys just looked at me. Then I began to hear some grumblings.

    "What the fuck was that?" one person asked.

    "Did he just diss us?" asked another. They started to laugh at me.

    "Buddy, you on some whole other weird shit," one person said to me. "Who do you think you are Common or somebody?" They continued to laugh as the Southbound train came, and they got on. I wasn't too upset because I thought I did pretty well. Maybe if I rapped about something I didn't have, they'd loved it. As I sat back down on the bench, the old man stood up and starting clapping.

    "I don't listen to a lot of that hip-hop stuff," he said, "but that right there was poetry. I think you did better than all of them."

    "Thank you," I replied.

    "So where ya headed?" he asked.

    "I'm not quite sure," I said. "I'm just travelin'. I know it's something or someplace out there for me, I just don't know where it is. But I'm going to find it." The old man sat back down.

    "Yeah, I hear ya, Youngblood," he said. "You know, I lot of people try and run away to find something. But if they don't know where they're going, they'll be lost forever. Let me ask you a question, did you look inside yourself first?" I shrugged.

    "What do you mean?"

    "Well, son, you gotta look at you first before you look at anything else. If there's a dream inside of you, you need to find out what verbs you need to do to turn that dream into reality. A thought is just one verb away from reality. And travelin' may not be the verb for you. Maybe it's another action, like being. Being is the most important verb around, because if you know how to be, then you already know how to do. Then, son, you can do anything." As he said that, the Northbound train arrived. "Well, I hope you find what you're looking for," he said, and then he turned and hopped on the train. He left me with a lot to think about. So I kneeled down at the bench and said a short prayer myself. However, halfway into the prayer, a bright light shined into my eyes, nearly blinding me. I couldn't see for a while, so I rubbed my eyes real hard, and then reopened them. When I reopened them, I was in a different place. Everything was so bright around me. The colors illuminated of the walls, as the floor lit up every time I stepped. I was still at the train station, but I saw everything in a different light. I saw how everything could look if I stayed to help change it. I was no longer in the Land of the Sleepwalkers, I was in another realm. I had finally awakened.

LISTEN: BE YOU!

Do you remember me?

I'm that old thought in your head begging you to be free?

Remember when I told you not to follow the crowd?

Always be yourself and never let anyone hold you down?

Yeah you didn't listen, did you?

Now you're a clone,

Half-somebody else and half-your own,

Don't even know who you are sometimes,

They've broken you into two,

And now you're so divided,

Even if I multiplied it you still wouldn't be one,

Because half of you and half of other folks

Only equals to make you a zero, a joke.

They know you're fake so they don't really respect you,

There's no real love so you feel as if they neglect you,

You could've surrounded yourself with friends

That'll love you for you,

But instead of listening to me,

You decided to do what others do.

Mm…

It's a shame too,

Because the thing you didn't realize is,

The whole time everyone you was trying to be

Was really wishing they could be like you.

I tried to tell you!

But you didn't listen.

LOOK AT HIM!!!!(GOD)

Look at me today!!
When worlds collide,
When thought patterns shift from their parallel state,
Crashing into each other,
Mind so confused that the demon on one shoulder
And the angel on the other both sound right
And you don't know what to do,
Look at me!!
When your day becomes dark,
The moon shoots flames from its crescent,
Stars stab your sun like daggers,
Supernovas pierce through your clouds,
Causing a storm so strong it feels as if
It's raining cats and dogs literally,
When the fog is so thick you can't see,
Stop looking at the situation and just
Look at me!!
I know your heart's desire is not to be fed to the wolves,
Your love trampled upon by the herd,
Your needs mocked by the hyenas,
Your screams for grace never heard,
Why put on boxing gloves to fight the sharpshooter?
Why sit on the train tracks of turmoil,
The 7:45 speeding towards your soul,
Faster and faster with no brakes,
This locomotive is out of control!
What are you going to do?
Allow yourself to be crushed in the midst?

No!

Don't worry about that train on the tracks,

Or the knifes in your back,

The vultures that swarm will not feast today,

All those things which are not beneficial to your salvation

Will go away!

Just close your eyes,

And look at me today.

A NATURAL REMEDY

When they told me I was wrong cuz I didn't like that song,
When they told me I was weird cuz I didn't want diamonds in my ears,
When they told me I would be in a cell cuz everyone around had failed.
All I did was laugh,
HA HA HA HA HA!!!!
When they told me that my dreams wouldn't mean a thing,
When they told me I should try to do other things,
When they told me I was foul cuz I didn't follow the crowd,
All I did was laugh,
HA HA HA HA HA!!!!
See,
I told you I lived in a different town,
Where dreams didn't come from textbooks,
They lived amongst the clouds,
And when doubt and unbelief comes to tear you down
Everybody laughs,
HA HA HA HA HA!!!!
See,
I'm from a land where being different
Helps you make a difference,
And since that's the understanding there is no indifference,
So no matter who you are you can still have your spirit lifted
All you have to do is laugh,
HA HA HA HA HA!!!!
So when they tell you that you're strange cuz you believe in change,
When they say that you are crossed cuz you are your own boss,
When they say that you are bugged cuz you show love to everyone,

Just do what my town does,
HA HA HA HA HA!!!!

Laughter is a natural remedy.

OUTCASTIN'

Taken aback by the loud echoes,
He decided to remain an outcast.
Because when you're on the outside looking in,
It's sort of like watching the world replay on film,
Seeing the same mistakes reiterated again and again,
And this replay stays on repeat,
Because all of the insiders want to accomplish the same feat.
This, amazingly, is usually just defeat,
But when you're defeated as a fleet,
It seems to make all the sour times so sweet,
That's why when things are so despicable in the hood.
Folk just chalk it up to it being "all good"
They have the talent and skills to do more than
Just merely pay the bills,
But instead of getting the ball moving,
They just sit still.
Obviously, they're not sick and tired of
Poverty and depression's ills,
And if they are it seems as if they can be healed,
By a cigarette, and brew, and a pill.
But seeing the repeated mistakes of those in the present,
Being presented with an option but opting to do
What the other insiders did in the past,
He decided to remain on the opposite side of the glass,
He decided to remain an outcast,
And from the bottom of his heart he can honestly say
As an outcast,

I'm glad.

EBONY TREES

Sitting near the shore,
Sipping on a tall glass
Of all the tears that poured
Down the faces if the Ebony Trees
That provides shade for me.
I glance out upon the ocean's waves
That stands tall like Heaven's gates,
Only to come crashing down like the towers
If they don't like the God we praise,
Or the children we raised,
Or the oil prices we paid,
Shoot, you pick the reason!
And I know that both joy and pain
Will have their season,
But 12 months of winter
Almost had me not believing,
But finally,
After the coldness of winter
And the storms of spring,
Thru the melting snow I saw specks of green,
And when the temperature stopped dropping,
My hopes began to rise,
And when the sun rose
It stared deeply into my eyes,
It burned for a second
And I couldn't see,
But when the pain went away,
I looked up,

And saw a different side of me.
A better side,
One whose shine would illuminate the dark,
And the sun was so bright
It even illuminated my heart,
The sunshine even drew me into
The place where I now stand,
Where lies and strife
Are burned at the stake
And truth is in high demand.

The trees and vegetation
Are made up from a nation
That kneeled and prayed
For a lost generation,
They shoved their roots into the ground
So that they would not be swayed,
So that if we just get past the dark winter,
We'd see plenty of brighter days,
And that nation formed the tree
That I now sit under for shade
So that I won't get burned when heat
Decides to come my way,
I drank their tears for I understand
And that understanding gives me strength
So when I see autumn in the air,
Instead of tearing down,
I can uplift.
When 9/11 or Katrina happens
And some hearts turn cold

Or filled with greed,
I can in turn give shade
To a friend in need.

Sitting near the shore,
Sipping on a tall glass
Of all the tears that poured
Down the faces of the Ebony Trees
That provides shade for me.
With my eyes on the shore,
And with my glass in my hand,
I can smile
Because I finally understand.

INFINITE LIMITLESS

I AM.
I AM INFINITE.
I AM LIMITLESS.

I am forever growing,
A snowball effect of greatness
Barreling down on an unsuspecting town
Like an avalanche hitting Fresno in June,
Yet I bloom like Jasmines
On a warm summer afternoon.

I am forever knowing,
I am the envy of the dictionary
And the most hated by Britannica,
Summa cum laude in the heart,
Valedictorian on the streets of Atlanta,
I drank the sap from the Poplar Trees
That bore the strange fruit Billie Holiday sang about,
And from that I gained the knowledge
Of my ancestors who wasn't
Allowed to read,
Yet still invented things that
You wouldn't believe.

I am forever showing,
Signs and visions of a better living,
Crafted by God and gained by wisdom,
The hopes and dreams of men and women

Who see the light yet are
Surrounded by darkness,
They can't see the roadmap on their journey,
They got lost on the highway to happiness,
So they are always yearning,
Itching for a chance
To make it to the dance,
They have a dream but
They don't have a plan.
I say to them,
Follow God,
He'll understand,
And lead you on the right path
To the Promised Land.

I am forever flowing,
Like the Rio Grande or the Nile,
Blood flowing like the Red Sea
Into my lower abdomen,
So I'm ready to give the world
My child,
My seed,
So everyone can birth
Intellectual, free-spirited,
Metaphorical babies,
Not real children of course,
But seed to help them believe,
To help them achieve
Mentally, spiritually,
Financially and physically,

Therefore if my flow is just right,
You might just birth a new idea tonight.

I am forever whole,
I am everything and anything
I have ever wanted to be,
Because thru Him
I know who I am,
And there is no stopping me.

I AM INFINITE.
I AM LIMITLESS.
I AM.

THE INGENIOUS RAMBLINGS

They saw me and said, "he's different",
They heard me and thought "he's weird",
I was never understood
By many of my peers,
They saw me smile and asked "what's wrong?"
They saw me frown and cheered,
But when I stared expressionless,
I was their worst fear,
Sometimes I tried to please them,
To be apart of the clique,
But as I walked my feet would hurt
Because that shoe didn't fit,
So I decided to be myself,
And they thought I'd gone mad,
But when I was in your so-called insanity
That was when I was glad.
I was never like you,
And was a fool to try to be,
But it all made sense when I saw you
Struggling to be like me,
You wish you could be yourself,
But you've become a clone,
So you follow the crowd so much
That you have no footsteps of you own,
Now you see me as someone that's free,
But you don't know who you are,
As my thought patterns create galaxies,
While you struggle to be a star,

So while you play the 3rd Tenor
In an orchestra singing the same old song,
It'll just be me and G.O.D. as my thoughts
Ramble On.
The Ingenious Ramblings of A Madman

RAMBLE ON, YOUNG MAN

Well, I am no longer in the Land of the Sleepwalkers. I am now living in Perfect Peace. I didn't have to buy a plane ticket or a bus pass or anything of that nature. All I had to do was WAKE UP. Losing my job was probably the best thing that happened to me. It took me out of my comfort zone and forced me to deal with reality, and that reality was the fact that I was wasting my gifts and talents cutting meat. I should've been taking my Journal of Rambled Thoughts and sharing them with the world. Sunshine needs to hear my thoughts, and the owner of the Hotel needs my words to help rekindle his passion. The truths in my mind could've kept Mr.G-Man from that big, white lie. My rambled thoughts are like Hershey Kisses; they were meant to be unwrapped and enjoyed, not locked away in a cupboard to spoil. Everything you go through is a lesson that'll help you turn your thoughts into a precious reality.

So, I finally understand that what I was searching for was a purpose in life, and that purpose was inside me all along. There was no need for me to physically travel, but I needed to mentally travel. I needed to take my mind on a journey within myself to truly understand my destiny. Once I understood my destiny, no longer did I look upon my world as an eyesore. Instead, I saw the true potential this world really has, and how God wants this world to be. So now I can affect the world positively, rather than focus on the negativity. It's easy to look down on a situation when everybody around you is down. If you decide to look up, to look at the situation differently, then people think something is wrong with you. They think you're a madman. Who are you to look at the glass half full?

Ah, but that's the problem. When you are looking down upon a situation, is that really you? Are you really that negative, or have you let the negativity of those around you enter into you? Has that negative energy encompassed itself within your soul, suffocating your dreams and putting you into a deep, metaphorical sleep? Have you become a clone, or a zombie, just going thru the motions everyday, trapped inside the Land of the Sleepwalkers? If so, I have a challenge for you. WAKE UP.

It's time you've awoken and reinvigorated those thoughts and dreams within you. Put a verb with your thoughts and allow them to become your reality. Let your mind wonder outside of that old, clichéd box, for that's where the greatest ideas lie. Every great person that ever lived had to, at some point, allow his mind to ramble on, and they wrote down those rambles, and allowed God to turn those rambling thoughts into a revived reality. Don't allow your wildest thoughts and dreams to stay in the wild. Let your mind travel into the wildest corners of your imagination and grasp those thoughts and dream, and turn them into your reality.

For every kid with a dream and every adult that think it's too late to dream, I say this to you; ramble on, young man. Ramble on.

Other UnLabeled Entertainment Releases

ETCHED IN STONE:
A COLLECTION OF THE SPOKEN WORD
Released October 2005

THE SUBLIME WOMAN PROJECT
2008 CALENDER AND PHOTOBOOK
Released December 1st, 2007

Available at www.lulu.com/mirakuluz1

Coming soon

EYES ON THE STREET
THE NOVEL

HOOD HERO
THE RAP MIXTAPE

FATE
THE CARTOON

For information on these releases and other future projects please visit the following websites:

www.TheUnLabeled.talkspot.com

www.myspace.com/Mirakuluz

www.lulu.com/mirakuluz1

For booking Mirakuluz, comments, or questions please contact us at

Mirakuluz1@hotmail.com

ABOUT THE AUTHOR

Mirakuluz (born Johnny Conley) is a poet, author, rapper, songwriter and photographer born and raised in Atlanta, GA. He has been writing songs and poetry since he was in elementary school. He first began to record music as a teenager as a member of a five-member rap group. After graduating from South Atlanta High School in 2000, he attended West Georgia University to study English and Photography. While in college, he regained a love for spoken word and began to perform at several facilities and functions throughout the Southeast. He released his first poetry book, Etched In Stone, in 2005. He now currently runs multimedia company UnLabeled Entertainment, and he is working on several new projects. He still lives in Atlanta, and has a six-year old son.

www.ingramcontent.com/pod-product-compliance
Lightning Source LLC
Chambersburg PA
CBHW032022040426
42448CB00006B/708